# *Mushroom Tea*

## The Poetry of Erika Joyce

© 2011, Erika Joyce.

Material may not be reprinted or reproduced without prior written permission.

Published by CTS Publishing, New York, NY

# Mushroom Tea

## Table of Contents

| | |
|---|---|
| Freedom .......................... 1 | Time Zone ....................... 33 |
| Tree of Life ...................... 2 | Boudicca ........................ 34 |
| The Shiny Vase ................... 3 | Shadows ......................... 35 |
| Champagne Mist .................. 4 | Taken ........................... 36 |
| The Other Sides .................. 5 | Mushroom Tea ................... 37 |
| Flying Orange .................... 6 | Bliss ............................ 38 |
| Moonlight Lust ................... 7 | Innocence ....................... 39 |
| The Tunnel ...................... 8 | The Equalizer ................... 40 |
| Kahlua and Talulah ............... 9 | Moonlight ....................... 41 |
| The Big Apple ................... 10 | Compassion ..................... 42 |
| Maternal Love ................... 11 | Mermaid ........................ 43 |
| Peace Within .................... 12 | In the Moment .................. 44 |
| No Regrets ...................... 13 | Life ............................. 45 |
| Memories ....................... 14 | Juices Flow ..................... 46 |
| Little Tabby ..................... 15 | Rotation ........................ 47 |
| Beast and Beauty ................ 16 | Elusive Love .................... 48 |
| Tango Vamp ..................... 17 | Another Day .................... 49 |
| Rejoice ......................... 18 | Altered States ................... 50 |
| Sated Glow ...................... 19 | The Dancing Spider .............. 51 |
| Bound By Blood .................. 20 | Bottomless ...................... 52 |
| Comfortable Silence .............. 21 | In Flight ........................ 53 |
| Dark Chocolate .................. 22 | Salty Seas ....................... 54 |
| On The Edge .................... 23 | Glass Slippers ................... 55 |
| Time ........................... 24 | That Night ...................... 56 |
| Piece of Heaven ................. 25 | Touch .......................... 57 |
| Primal Dance .................... 26 | Presence ........................ 58 |
| Perseverance .................... 27 | Reverie ......................... 59 |
| True Heart ...................... 28 | That Place ...................... 60 |
| Pagan Gifts ..................... 29 | Another Leap ................... 61 |
| Transition ...................... 30 | Shedding Skin ................... 62 |
| Weres and Vamps ................ 31 | Winter Wonderment ............. 63 |
| Contemplate .................... 32 | Sweet Solitude .................. 64 |

I am dedicating my book of poems to my husband, Frank, who always encouraged me, believed in me and stood by me; even when he found me still writing at dawn. His undying faith in me was unwavering, even when I was talking to myself at the dinner table.

I also dedicate my book to my muse, my cousin Angelo, an established and talented poet. After reading one of his books, I have not been able to stop writing.

Thank you, Frank. Thank you, Angelo.

# *Foreword*

My poems have come from within. I hope they reach your heart and soul, and delve into the meaning and sometimes, the absurdity of it all. Allow yourself to be taken on emotional journeys, erotic escapades, flights of fancy, and most importantly, a tickling of your funny bone.

# *Freedom*

Clouds as thick and white as Highland wool,
Whirl about misty moors.
Horses run free through fragrant open fields.
While a ball of sun peeks through the veil.
Pungent greenery and sweet heathered paths
Lead the way to a pub by the sea.
Dark ale flows fluidly.
A crackling fire and a dram of whiskey
Warms the soul.
And of course, the melodic voice of a bonnie lass
Singing stories of a time long past
Music vibrates through the air
People laugh, dance, and sing songs of long ago.
When tribes of blue faced warriors roamed
Through the fields. Hungry and wounded,
Cloaked in little more than bravery and pride,
Became the most legendary poets
Of such great land.

## *Tree of Life*

I pick an apple from a tree.
And sink my teeth deliberately.
Sweet juice drips on my chin.
Lips start to form a grin.
Thirst quenching and crispy sweet,
Savoring every bite, to the core.
I place the seeds in the ground
And tenderly cover them all around.
Now time to say a pagan prayer
More apples will come back
Some other year.

## *The Shiny Vase*

Handed down through time and space,
My mother gave me a shiny vase –
Tall and proud upon it's' stand;
I see dancing crystals of another land.
Although I'm told it's only glass,
I hear a soft, melodic voice –
Gran's smiling eyes filled with love,
Her wise and lovely face.
Patrician hands, rough from work and toil,
To me, the vase is diamonds of grace.

## *Champagne Mist*

Sweet mist and flying clouds
Quench the thirst of open fields.
Greedy roots with giant hands
Suck in all the moisture that they can.
Violet heather tangos with pungent greens
Water wells replenish to the max.
And streams race so very fast
Crackling fireplaces all ablaze.
Large drops tumbling on windowpanes
The lazy sun continues to hide behind fragrant hills.
A soft glow emerges to tease and play.
Today the champagne mist is here to stay.

## *The Other Sides*

What lies beneath the placid pond?
The come hither smile upon the lake,
A wink of an eye upon the reflective face.
Promises of a land,
So very far beyond;
Where wishes and dreams
Do not just play upon the mind.
Fragrant petals cushion and pave the floor.
Flowers forever bloom while seagulls loom.
Tides wash up pearls and jewels upon the shore.
Who could ask for more?
The frothy spray of organza mist
Intoxicates you into a state of total bliss.
A path in the forest goes on and on.
Funneled trees lead to an august land
Of mystery and romance.
Nuzzle with the wilds of the unknown,
Like snuggling doves.
Crimson cardinals congregate overhead.
The melodic sound in the atmosphere
Inebriates from ears to toes.
Behind the wall, the darkened forest,
The brilliant light beyond the green grassy hedge,
What of the reflection in the mirror down the hall?
When the wild calls,
Fly the nest with hungry abandon
And total zest.

## *Flying Orange*

The sun was high, the wind was still,
A bird perched on a windowsill.
Gently, gingerly, I placed a small orange slice.
With a twitch of the head and a flick of the wing,
Off goes the orange in a feathery flight.

## *Moonlight Lust*

Breathing labored; rapid heartbeat.
Dizzying sweat drips.
The night is hot.
Pressure and passion
Build a little too fast.
Soon it will be dawn.
The sensation will not last.
Fret not, the moon's still high,
The night's still young.
Hypnotic love, lust, hunger –
Thirst!
Tomorrow, the moonlight will come,
Once again.

## *The Tunnel*

Lurking shadow in the corner –
Friend or foe?
Piercing eyes in the dark,
Soft and comforting.
Sometimes penetrating to the bone.
A voice in the night,
Objects go missing;
Then return.
Covers adjusted around my shoulders;
Legs get chilled, and then catch fire.
Music of another time and place,
I start to move and sway.
Caught in an undulating tunnel
Of desire and despair
And then it goes away.

# *Kahlua and Talulah*

I once knew a cat named Kahlua,
Who fell in love with a mouse named Talulah!
Complacent as a cat can be,
"Come away with me; we'll live by the sea, eternally!"
Talulah thought this peculiar.
She would not submit;
Not quite ready to commit.
Such a considerate cat was he,
Swept up his beloved
In a cozy little spot between sharp teeth.
Talulah started to feel warm and fuzzy.
Flying on a magic carpet, special delivery.
So she hitched a ride to the sea.
The rhythmic rocking and swaying
Was quite stimulating,
As multiple orgasmic as a little mouse could be.
After tiring a bit, Kahlua stopped
For a nice bowl of cream.
Feeling a bit dizzy, Talulah started to stagger and sway;
"Splendid!" thought Kahlua, what a nice time to play!
Tossed in the air again and again,
Next, a bath, on the agenda –
Talulah, ever so ready to surrender,
Nice, long strokes of a warm, prickly tongue
As deep in a trance as can be.
With a lick and a nibble, and a large gulp,
Down, down went she.
Kahlua as content as can be
"Now we are one, forever and ever,"
Basking in the sun,
Licking paws and biting between toes,
A short walk was now in order.
The litter box awaiting special delivery.
So goes the story of eternity
Between Kahlua and Talulah.

## *The Big Apple*

So many spaces;
Anonymous faces,
Magnetic seduction.
You do as you please,
By day or by night.
The Apple has choices -
Waxing mundane, organic
Or wormy.
The pulsating pull leads you
To your journey.

# *Maternal Love*

A round ball of flesh,
All soft and delicious.
Innocent of life.
Everything's so new.
Air, light, curiosity.
Fear.
But, Momma is always near.
He snuggles in closely,
Showing off gums with smiling delight.
She licks his forehead,
Nibbles his toes.
Momma, so strong, soft, enticingly sweet.
Time to feed from round, pretty breasts.
Baby grows quickly –
Developing muscle and mind.
The bond becomes stronger and stronger.
Maternal passion, proud possession,
All wrapped up safely in one.

## *Peace Within*

A child's anxious scream –
A desperate cry.
Tenderly, I scoop her up;
She clings with all her might.
I rest my chin on her precious
Pumpkin head.
She snuggles to my chest
As if in a protective pouch or nest.
Sweet orange hair
And peachy skin;
Surrounded by chatter,
I do not hear a thing.
Shared comfort flows,
As breath unites.
Within a crowded room,
We share a private peace within.

## *No Regrets*

A stone tossed into a mountain lake,
Spreads currents of circular swirls.
The shiny glare continues on.
A touch can send chills, thrills and signals
To the brain. Embedded.
Then memory starts to wane.
A word or two can make or break a day,
Although they fade away.
A swing continues to sway
As a child naps after play.
Fleeting moments come and go
Joy and pain register in the deepest recess
Of the mind and soul.
Sun rises, sun sets, time spirals on
With no regrets.

## *Memories*

A sudden sound, but nothing's there;
The glimpse of a shadow,
In the corner of an eye.
Is it music?
Or a pleasant voice?
Holding clothes close to the face,
Familiar scent,
A warm caress,
Memories endure, images can fade.
Person, place or time,
Embedded in the mind.

# Little Tabby

Flower buds awaken, to the soft melody of birds.
Little tabby licks her paws, washes her face,
Bathed by the warm spring sun.
We eat lunch together, and chat.
Each with our own primal sounds.
The bond is so strong, we snooze in
The warmth of the sun.
I wake to the twilight and stretch every muscle,
While little tabby sleeps on...

## *Beast and Beauty*

The temperament and beauty was quite mesmerizing.
And asked ever so politely if I could stop to admire,
With a pat on the head, a few kind words,
We exchanged such good vibrations.
So big, white and hairy, and weighed more than me.
The temperament of a saint, the beauty of a madonna.
Decided to take a chance and asked to take a photo
of such a magnificent creature.
Much to my surprise, there was a beast
at the other end of the leash.
As brusquely as can be, he said, "Piss off."
I smiled brightly and nodded
At such stupidity.
Told him his dog was more charming and intelligent than he.
While walking away, I felt sorry for such a pitiful person.
Once again, to my surprise, I felt a tear drip from my eye.
And started to cry.

# *Tango Vamp*

Lead me so very far away.
Don't let me find my own way.
Danger – ecstasy have morphed into one.
Salivating desperately for my forbidden fruit
Soon I know the moon will sink.
I take the flower from my hair
And hold it tightly to my breast
While I return to my place of rest.
And when the moon become full bloom,
You and I shall rendezvous.
Eternal dance through the sky,
Just until the sun shall rise.

## *Rejoice*

Grasp every pleasure with total abandon
As never before
Eat chocolate, sing, drink and dance 'til you drop.
Eternity, the end of time as we know it
Do not wait 'til rebirth
Feel the earth, so rich with both hands.
Inhale the air as deeply as you can.
Jump into water and fly through the fire.
Exult!
Today is the end and beginning of the rest of your life.

## *Sated Glow*

Pulsating, contracting,
Slippery smooth.
Gripping and pulling
Swelling with pungent, nectarous ooze.
Stormy, volcanic desires are soothed.
Just a quick rest
Before desperate needs once again,
Start to flow.
Two bodies connected
In one shimmery, sated glow.

## *Bound By Blood*

Desperately reaching to the moon
Soaring high above thick dark mist
Dancing and weaving safely through flaming stars
Deep below earth and sea
When fiery sun starts to glow.
As time goes on, most will die;
Others dance and fly
To another place, space and time.
Bound by blood
Time to feed.
Come be my mate.

## *Comfortable Silence*

We held hands while walking and talking,
Sharing ideas.
We held hands while walking, not talking,
Sharing our time.
We held hands while walking in silence,
An occasional word.
A walk with communication,
The most meaningful kind.

## *Dark Chocolate*

Sensual pleasures run rampant while cooking.
Steaming, sautéing, chopping, and blending.
Flavor and texture moving around the tongue,
Seductively become one.
Tasting and sampling can be so alluring.
Chewing, nibbling swallowing slowly
Savoring every bite.
Licking dark chocolate off fingers,
Rich and so smooth.
A digestive of brandy or cognac
Will help comfort and seal in the mood.

## *On The Edge*

Tides roll in, tides roll out,
Magnetic moonlight flows through the night
Round, bright orb watches as we tease and play.
A lick, a nibble, a small, tender bite
Gently welding until a morning cascade of birds
Serenade with lusty delight.
Cool wind blows from the beach below.
Sensual sensations unknown;
Whispers upon earlobes, gentle strokes on flesh,
Tides change course, gusty winds moan.
Drunken blood and sweat pulsates.
Frantic, famished thrusts of desperate love,
Salivating kisses, fevered, glistening skin,
Moonlight gravity has morphed.
Greedy needs lie deep within.

## *Time*

Love me, don't leave me.
I want you to stay.
Youth starts to wane,
As leaves blow away.
Seasons change, flowers bloom,
Roots are embedded
While embellishments stray.
So love me with passion.
Take me before I go.
Memories are rooted and
Infinitely grow.

## *Piece of Heaven*

Soft, white sand stretched out
While looming seagulls send
Signals to a friend.
A sailboat lingers,
A fish jumps with pleasure.
Children laugh and play by the shore.
Young lovers walk hand in hand,
While other people snore.
Couples apply lotion,
While caressing the skin.
A loner watches before taking a swim.
Waves tease the shoreline,
Delivering seashells and seaweed.
A scavenger's delight!
The sun starts to wane
With nice cooling breezes –
A little piece of heaven!
Hungrily, the sea swallows
That great ball of light.

## *Primal Dance*

When you lead me, I follow you.
A liberating transfer of the will.
A door left opened,
You read my mind,
I take your cue.
The Tango communication...
Souls weld, bodies melt, and hearts speak a private, primal language.
Just for me, just for you.

## *Perseverance*

After a rainfall, Sydney the spider starts mending his web.
Contemplating delectable delights, dangling on a thread.
Sydney's last catch, juicy, yet chewy did not really last.
Flies – crunchy, fruity and sweet – a very nice treat
Spicy beetles, nice and meaty, give poor Sydney gas.
High protein, industrious ants, always so quick to scurry –
Small, yet good when you're in a hurry.
Released from confinement,
The influx of moths and butterflies so light and moist
Result in digestive reflux.
Laboriously working on a strong additional sleeve,
Hoping a centipede will fall into his weave.
Humming a Screaming Jay Hawkins tune,
Pondering his next prey;
First a bite, before falling into a spell,
Then dragged into a funneled tunnel.
While stalking Anita the ant, his latest desire,
He slips through his web,
And falls on his head;
With unbridled persistence,
Sydney starts mending his web once again.

## *True Heart*

We breathed the same air,
A long time ago.
Your face, still clear through distance and time.
So many years can change the mind.
But the heart stays true.
As if, you were still mine.

## *Pagan Gifts*

A succulent apple dangling from a tree,
Ready to be plucked.
Let it stay until it falls away
So ripe, round, juicy sweet and shiny red!
Feast your eyes while juices flow.
Pagan gifts always come back
And then they go.

## *Transition*

The plight of a new vampire
A challenge not to be believed.
Stronger than human,
Weaker than my colleagues.
An ex-vegetarian must go out and feed,
The blood tastes putrid,
Food dyes, inoculations, preservatives and prescriptives.
Old timers tell me of a time long a go
Air smelled clean and humans were delectable.
Virgins in great abundance, the sweetest of treats.
One night, my maker taught me a wonderful skill.
Not all my donors quite willing to stay still,
One bat of an eyelash, a victims' ready to serve.
A hypnotic trance so easily induced!
My teacher, an ancient Viking from a time long past,
Tall, blond, so incredibly fast; can fly, dive
And even change form.
His intoxicating blood, so strong, so sweet,
An occasional treat.
He promised to fly me to a land
Where humans are still succulent, sweet meat.
A long flight so I must strengthen, hydrate and lubricate.
And continue my feat.
No ticket lines, no pat down, no electronic scans.
My skin smooth and dewy, sinuous muscle,
Taut and so tight.
No skin creams, no wasted days at the gym;
Just a deep slumber before my search
For nocturnal delights.
Turned in time, so ripe – clinging to my youth
Now, no aches, no pains, eternally young.
So lovely, cloaked in my new gift -
A red velvet cape, ready to hunt.
Sounds like a real stroke of luck,
But sometimes it really does suck.

## *Weres and Vamps*

So dark, yet so bright,
The mysteries of the night!
Voluptuous full moon,
Scintillating starlight –
An owl hoots softly.
Creatures of darkness –
Some hairy and hot,
Others cold, pale –
So white!
People take cover,
While others swell
With joy and delight.

## *Contemplate*

Grace, youth and strength,
In perfect harmony.
Sinuous muscle, strong necks with long burly legs.
Powerful arms branch from strapping torsos,
Like towering, v-shaped trees.
Kissed by the angels and blessed by the gods.
With the speed of a panther,
The agility and beauty of a bird in flight.
Eyes try to separate as one darts left
And the other darts right.
The soccer ball in full flight.
The field speckled with a visual feast for all the senses.
Adrenaline rush on both sides of the fence.
Pried away by my lovely young niece and told,
"You have looked enough, now time to go eat."
I go with regret, although appetite has peaked
Heading off for a very strong drink.
Such a sight can make a girl think.

# *Time Zone*

Waiting, anticipating – looking at the door.
Reading a menu, which has not been read before.
No waiter, no patrons,
Hot coffee, no food.
Watching your reflection in the window
While passing by the store,
Wearing a dress never seen before.
Reading yesterday's newspaper again;
Waiting for a train that never comes.
Opening a window that's never been closed before
Grasping for the phone in silent hesitation
Standing by the bureau, watching the clock;
While a suit waits, hanging on a door...
Getting out of bed;
Have I slept the night before?
Frozen in motion, as if in a dream,
A painting, another dimension,
A frame of time unexplained
Implanted in the mind,
Another place, another zone
Perhaps another time.

## *Boudicca*

Boudicca, the beauteous red tabby
Breaks so many hearts.
Deliberately stretching her most enticing parts.
Such grace, such agility!
Sprawled on a soft, unmade bed.
The best kind of bed;
With nooks, waves and crannies,
Designed for the sheer pleasure
Of snuggling, licking, salivating,
So conspicuously content.
An orange, red velvet coat probed and lubricated
With a long, prickly tongue.
Furry hands and feet taste best
When dipped into pink, perky ears.
Not to mention the tickling of whiskers
On clandestine, moist places.
Reaching the highest of plateaus,
A romance from lashes to toes.
Basking on the sunny side of her throne
Clouds part on command.
Suddenly, a meandering tom picks up
On the plumes of Boudicca's scintillating fumes.
While exposing her round little belly,
She hisses a guttural groan;
With a flick of an ear and a twitch of her nose,
She turns away, revealing the most enticing of tails.
"My regal lineage, so noble, so royal
Dates back centuries ago.
Who are you?
Prowling, rummaging –
You belong in a zoo!"

# *Shadows*

A dark, frothy cloud rolls in,
Intruding on my space within.
Shadow moving through the wall,
Falling timbers burn my skin and soul.
Dark waters rushing all about;
Painfully creeping up my legs.
As sweat drips from my forehead,
Mirrors beckoning me to step right through
To another side and place.
Lurking shadows continue to permeate my space.
Running frantically to lock the door,
Rocking back and forth
In my safety nest, while hugging knees
Tightly to my chest.
Nestling branches – hold on tight
While I try to breathe with all my might.

## *Taken*

Taken away while so vital and young,
So hard to grasp when youth flows so freely
Through mist and wind.
Vitality, spontaneity and verve.
Such energy makes the sun rise and fall.
Young hearts spin and mourn
A profound loss of optimistic innocence.
So hard to stay aground,
Feeling trapped within a maze.
Sometimes the haze begins to lift;
Memories continue so far and so long,
As waves can rise and trees can grow.
Held on shoulders, secure and safe;
Undulating waves thrash and crash.
Long arms and legs,
Eyes as blue as the sky above.
Holding onto a nice, shiny bald head,
Chest hair as orange as the sunshine,
And the child held high aloft.
A small freckled face, with huge eyes
Turns toward devouring,
Rampaging waves, moving forward.
Never frightened. Not a single fear.
Long arms would sooner separate
And flow out to sea
Before ever being dropped
Beneath such enormous energy.
Suddenly taken so far away,
With no time to say the things
A person needs to convey.
A divine revelation washes over me
Infinity
Another time, another place- perhaps a predetermined plan.
A humble prayer whispers deeply
In my mind and soul.
Life's flow infinitely continues
as the depth and breadth of the deep blue sea.

# Mushroom Tea

Damp chill and rain all through the night;
It may be spring, lusty winds continue to fight.
Rain knocks on windowpanes
As wilting fires wane.
Chimneys cough up winter's malaise,
Gusts of wind crash the old back yard fence.
Leaving a wide open space;
An invitation for spring to come…
A long, languid stretch while drinking morning tea;
Walking to the window to have a peek at what there is to see.
The mushroom haze begins to lift, birds flying overhead,
Trees reaching up with thirsty, greedy hands.
Nostrils fill with a pleasant scent of melted snow,
Pungent greens and newly budding blooms,
Water wells start to overflow;
As champagne drips from the sky to deep below,
Sunshine struggles to start the day.
Flowers blossom before my eyes.
Tantalizing tulips tango around a wishing well.
Marigolds mambo merrily.
Rabbits spring into a Lindy hop.
Cherry blossoms join in coyly, a bit reserved;
Suddenly, without warning burst into dancing the bachata
With total abandon and joy.
Lilies and lilacs love to stare, rhododendron rumba,
Pulsating spring romance is in the air.
A rainbow explodes above my head.
Champagne dripping from the sky saturates the air.
I levitate into the atmosphere, the ground soaks
And the party smokes.
Wisteria whisper sweet endearments.
Spring is here!

## Bliss

The softness of your lips when we kiss,
The firmness of your touch, dancing through the night;
Lips against my cheek, breath upon my ear,
Breathing deeply to catch your scent,
Swept off feet;
Floating on a cloud;
A summer lake;
A swirling bird in flight,
A higher level within my reach,
I hold on tight.
Spun in a web of total bliss,
When we kiss.

## *Innocence*

Urgently!
Racing to the top of the tree.
Higher and higher,
With long, spidery limbs.
A small child watches intensely,
With huge, hopeful eyes,
While sniffling and gulping for air.
Tears are wiped off freckled cheeks
With the back of her hand.
A big, red balloon –
The prized possession,
Is rescued, at last!
Chuckling a bit,
The kind-hearted aunt
Gracefully slinks down from the tree.
After a quick kiss and a hug,
The little freckle-faced girl runs off,
In joyful delight.
Watching such carefree innocence at play;
Her tattered new dress
Blows in the warm breeze
Of a lovely summer day.

# *The Equalizer*

Indigent. Indulgence.
Summer homes are renovated.
Swollen bellies from no food,
Shipped off to summer camps,
And sent away to private schools.
Broken water hydrants, over packed subways,
Struggling for air.
Horses, swimming, pottery, and plays;
Blood, switchblades, predatory gangs;
Fighting for rights.
Nannies picking up children.
Parents sail off on a cruise.
No father in sight,
Mother works two jobs,
In total despair.
Unsupervised recreation,
Or desperate survival.
Both sides shall meet.
When altered states are induced.
No discrimination here.
The grim reaper does not care.

## *Moonlight*

See the full moon then think of me.
Lush, ripe, so hot, hungry for you.
Touch me!
Kiss me!
Do as you will.
I take what I crave.
Memory holds true.

## *Compassion*

The softer the heart,
The thicker the skin grows.
Stoically, moving through the day.
See not, hear not;
But the heart turns to stone.
Searching deeply for my soul;
My skin starts to shed its' shell.
A sudden tear starts to well.
Compassion, once again,
Starts to flow.

# *Mermaid*

The winter scent flows off the North Sea.
Solitude, peace, romance, mystery.
Icebergs collide with silvery waves.
Whirling flakes dance seductively
Through mist, beckoning the mermaid in me.

## *In the Moment*

He loves me now, he loved me when.
She loved me then, now and again.
The sun is high; then sinks way below.
Chaste caterpillars crawl,
Butterflies mate, fly and never fall.
Sea tides change, washing in and riding out.
Homing pigeons fly west and then return,
Bearing messages, which soon will fade.
Beauty bursts, then changes form.
Leaves blow away, while roots endure.
Laughing with lusty abandon,
Eyes shed reflective tears.
Savoring moments that settle in to stay,
Until suddenly, they go away.
Youth comes and goes
As wisdom grows,
Capricious nature grows and flows.

# *Life*

Prancing angels around a waterfall,
Glittering staircase with bright shining light
Clean, fresh air,
Flower petals cushion every step.
A sudden chill penetrates to the marrow of my bone
I see a pond, all crystally clear.
Fluffy white clouds, singing birds a distance away.
The chill turns into an inferno of suffocating heat.
A stench of rot and decay,
I seem to have lost my way.
Dizzying confusion, little trolls taunt and tease,
I cannot breathe,
Clanking metal about to close.
While running away, I start to pray.
A sharp, excruciating pain shoots through my gut.
"Our Father who art in heaven."
Praying for redemption, promises I hope I can keep.
"Forgive us our trespasses, as we forgive those
who trespass against us?"
Metal crashes, breaking a rib,
Crawling like a serpent, fighting for air.
Suddenly, a comforting hand on mine, a serene coolness.
The pond returns, more beautiful than before.
Butterflies, violins, blooming trees.
A reprieve has been granted.
The warmth of a hand, familiar voices, soft murmurs,
Someone whimpers and cries.
So much to do, people who need me, memories start to flow.
I see a woman, she looks like me.
The light is fluorescent. So many tubes, a constant beeping.
"Wake up! Wake up!"
I want to come back,
But I'm caught in the wall.
No angels, no trolls,
Life.
I breathe, I cry,
I thank the Lord.

## *Juices Flow*

Insane sanity.
Roulette wheel whirls and twirls.
Never fails – outcome prevails.
Masses reign and never sway.
Nonconformists sing a tune
A more esoteric way.
Blinders can comfort
Diversities excite.
Creative juices flow
Without internal fights.

## *Rotation*

When I was young and you were old,
When you were young, I was old.
Time flies, the clock spins, planets rotate.
The repetition of life evolves.
Babies born, blossoms bloom,
Sunflowers face the sky, reaching high for the sun,
Until they wither and die.
Next year they sprout their smiling faces,
Reaching desperately to come full bloom.
Following the sun until it fades.
Snow once again, paves the hills and dunes.
Roads of no return as time wobbles and rotates
On its capricious pedestal.

## *Elusive Love*

It lurks. It stalks.
The sound I think I hear.
The shadow in the corner of my eye,
I turn my head, it disappears.
The breath upon my neck,
The whisper in my ear,
A brief reflection in the window,
Perhaps just the haze in the air.
Wind swirls as the sky starts to clear.
Hair is gently brushed from my forehead.
Was that the wind?
Now I feel your presence in the atmosphere.
Breathing deeply, my heart skips a beat.
Picking up your scent,
I feel your heat.
Your tender touch while I sleep,
Mouth moistens with a honeyed kiss.
When I wake, I smell your hair,
Taste your breath.
I wrap myself in sweetened sheets.
I feel your sweat.
You were here.

## Another Day

The twilight sky, creamy, smooth – a touch of pink.
A seductive tease – so far away.
Soon it will fade
Until the end of another day.

## *Altered States*

Tell me of a land so far away,
Where children play
Sun shines bright while diamond snowy crystals fall light
Mountains covered with angel dust
Rainbows reach across the expanse,
Land of mystery and romance.
Flowers burst with honeyed fumes
Large, winged birds in flight,
Hop upon a feathered nest.
Downy soft and fly through nectared mist.
Fill your lungs with sweetened air,
Catch the spray of cascading waterfalls
As you swirl, whirl and twirl
Lost in a dream, caught in a painting
Swimming in a glass of bubbly champagne
Surrender to altered states supreme.

# *The Dancing Spider*

Sitting by a window, knitting a sweater,
I noticed a spider spinning a web.
A sweater for warmth; a web for shelter and food.
How clever!
What an elegant dancer a spider can be.
Watching with admiration; dropping stitches,
Changing patterns, so intuitively.
Feeling inspired, I pulled out my stitches and
Created a pattern unique – just for me.
So much to learn from an eight-legged creature.
With a few more limbs, I could dance my way to a sweater
More elegantly.

## *Bottomless*

The bottomless wishing well;
Abundance, never to run out.
Some say the drains have clogged;
Prayers have lost their way
And simply float about.
One day will it overflow?
Or possibly run out?
Be assured, the bottom has yet to fall out.
Never empty, never overflows.
Needs and desires keep falling in,
As dreams and hopes fly out.

# *In Flight*

Come dance with me all through the night.
Lead me to ecstasy as we soar and dive like two birds in flight.
Pulsating music – adrenaline rush.
Arms turn into wings, and legs take flight.
Lead me to the flame of spinning temptation.
Trapped in a web of delight.

## *Salty Seas*

Waves rise and fall,
In vast, salty seas.
Sunlight is swallowed deep below
As freckled skies start to glow.
Sound and scent penetrate
Deeply within my heart and soul.
I shed my clothes
Limbs transform.
Clutching seaweed to my chest,
I retreat to the safety of my nest.

# Glass Slippers

They swell, throb, pulsate and sweat;
Some big and sturdy;
Others narrow and bony.
Nothing compares to a dancer's mangled mauled and malformed feet.
Some princes retreat when prying glass slippers on
Bunions, calluses and hammertoes at the end of long shapely legs.
The dancer can glide, slide and dive,
Whirl and twirl with the fluid agility and grace of a bird in flight.
And stilettos at the end of lovely, well-toned legs,
Are quite a mesmerizing sight.
Anti-inflammatories, cortisone injections, gels, bandages and tape
Can make the function of these feet a bit more complete.

## *That Night*

Remember that night so long ago,
Moon was high, brightening the sky.
Or was it just a filmy glare waiting to sink below?
That memorable night;
The warmth of fingers tingling skin
Lacy curtains so thin,
Allowing cool air to flow in.
Or did it rain?
Mind games tease and play
Upon my brain.
So warm that night, we held on tight.
As if we knew you would go so far away
That next day.
Deep slumber invites a reverie of magical delight.
Indulgent kisses, tastes and scents enter nostrils,
With welcoming consent.
Your voice vibrates deep in my ear canal,
In my sleep, my mind explodes.
Welding of mind body and soul.
Sharing our breath that night.
Waking upon my solitary bed,
Windows closed tightly the night before
Now wide opened
Enjoying cool, moist air,
Entering my atmosphere.
Starting just another day,
Waiting for your visit,
I start to pray.

## *Touch*

Don't touch we are told all through our youth
But why?
Touching makes you feel so incredibly good
Touch people you love.
A gentle caress.
Whether for passion, raging hormones, or caring for the old.
An old woman feels sexy and loved once again.
Her smile, the glimmer of a blossom in full bloom.
Old men feel a twinge of vitality and strength.
Memories of proms and dancing with girls.
Soft little babies feel comfort and safe,
And food, of course, tastes best when eaten with hands.
It starts with a scent. A touch, then a bite.
So touch a friend or a mate, a loving little squeeze
Will not intimidate.

## *Presence*

Walking through the park at dawn,
Your presence seems to drench the air.
Soft wind flows off a lake somewhere
Some say you have been reborn.
Perhaps you have changed your form.
Flowers bloom, while birds sing a lovely tune.
Sunshine warms the coolness of the morning air,
I feel the softness of your touch.
Your scent seems to permeate the atmosphere.
Is that your voice, or just the wind?
Eyes moisten with a salty tear,
Sometimes I think you may be near.

## *Reverie*

Holding a cup close to the lips,
Pondering.
Standing in a doorway,
So very still,
Contemplating.
Passing the looking glass
Inside an antique store,
Reflecting.
Approaching the Post Office,
Anticipating.
Reminiscing, while peering out a window
As clouds glide by.
Minutes
Hours
Years
Ruminating in deep reverie,
As time drifts by.

## *That Place*

How nice you look.
Do I know you?
Can't find my keys – Where's my car?
That fleeting moment in that secret place,
A few days, hours, years – a second or two;
A geometry equation solved that very same day;
Stories told of so very long ago,
Explicit details of an exquisite wedding day.
But what day is it today?
The forgotten name on the tip of the tongue,
The PIN number used again and again,
Looking for glasses when they're on your face,
Where do we go when memory becomes remiss?
Is it dark and dank? Do fires flare, burn the eyes?
Scorch the skin?
If this were true; why continue the journey back again
And then again?
Do we visit loved ones? A friend, a neighbor?
A favorite aunt? Perhaps a mate?
A place where angels play, sing and dance
While waiting on line to reserve your space?
Fragrant blossoms pave a path
Green hills run on and on
Long limbed trees reaching high
Rainbows forming ethereal beauty across the sky.
Suddenly a sigh illuminates –
Not Yet Your Time Follow the Petaled Path – Go Back.
One day our reservation will meet our special needs.
Only then is it time to take our place
In this customized space

## *Another Leap*

How do we know when love is true?
A light goes on and says "It's you".
Teetering on the top of the fence,
Take the leap, allow yourself to be swept off your feet.
If expectations do not reach the mountain tops in the sky,
The fence you leaped is not that high.

## Shedding Skin

If you were me
And I were you,
Would roles reverse?
Do old habits embed?
Always ingrained and stay true?
Crawling out of your skin and changing form,
Discomfort unfolds.
Minds expand when we break the mold.
Caterpillars, serpents, tadpoles just to name a few.
A great revelation beholds the unknown,
New outlooks awaken,
A metamorphosized you.

# *Winter Wonderment*

Crunching diamonds beneath my feet
Whistling winds nibbling on my cheeks
Lusty nibbles on ears and feet.
Glistening pearls collect on window sills;
Chimney fumes penetrate the diamond dust veil.
The pink and orange ball sinks behind rolling hills.
An owl hoots a persuasive song.
A shooting star sets the sky ablaze.
I run and slide through creamy drifts.
Seductive whirls lead me across a frozen lake.
A trail of glowing jewels set in snow,
Powerful pine trees with platinum arms
And emerald hands lift me off the frozen land.
Waves of winter wonderment intoxicate my heart and soul.

## *Sweet Solitude*

As I sit upon a rock
In the thicket of the woods,
Arms embrace me with lusty life.
Large trunks with thick growth
Shade my space;
Allowing just enough sun to warm my skin and face.
A fragrant sachet, a serenade of chirps and tweets;
A scurry – a flurry, a feathered flight.
No electronics to hinder the come hither call
Of wild life, wandering it's way through a blissful day.
Acorns and chestnuts pave the path
To a place which seems so far away.
Apples and berries, seductively sweet,
Whisper my name.
I close my eyes and say a silent pagan prayer –
Today, the gods are everywhere.

www.ingramcontent.com/pod-product-compliance
Lightning Source LLC
Chambersburg PA
CBHW051715040426
42446CB00008B/894